The Making of Mozart

Written by Ciaran Murtagh
Illustrated by John Dillow

Contents

Introduction	2
The beginning	4
Child genius on tour	8
Mozart's music	14
Doing things his way	20
Mozart's success	24
Glossary	28
Index	29
Young Mozart's diary	30

Collins

Introduction

You may not have heard of Wolfgang Amadeus Mozart, but you've probably heard his music. He died a long time ago, but people still enjoy listening to his work today.

Mozart's home today

Wolfgang Amadeus Mozart was a musician and **composer**. He was born in 1756 in the city of Salzburg in Austria. Mozart was a child genius.

By the age of three, he could play a **harpsichord**, and by the age of five, he was composing his own music. In his short life, he wrote more than 600 pieces of music. This is his story.

More on Mozart

Wolfgang was christened Johannes Chrysostomus Wolfgangus Theophilus Mozart. His family called him Wolfie or Wolferl for short.

The beginning

Wolfgang's father, Leopold, was a musician. Wolfgang's mother, Anna Maria, looked after him and his older sister Maria Anna, who the family called Nannerl.

When Wolfgang and Nannerl were growing up, only rich children could afford to go to school. Children from poor families worked on farms and in factories or helped their parents at work. Children who were somewhere in the middle, like Wolfgang and Maria Anna, were educated at home.

Mozart's home

Leopold taught his two children lots of subjects. His favourite was music. Because Leopold was also a composer, there were lots of musical instruments in their house. Wolfgang was lucky. Musical instruments were expensive and not many children were taught to play.

This is one of the musical instruments in Mozart's home.

One day, Leopold was teaching Maria Anna how to play an old-fashioned piano-like instrument called a harpsichord. When Leopold and Maria Anna had finished, Wolfgang hopped up to play too. He was only three years old. Everybody thought Wolfgang was too young to play. They were wrong.

Soon Wolfgang was playing just as well as Maria Anna. By the age of eight, he could play the organ and the violin too. Leopold realised his son was special and thought the world should know it.

Child genius on tour

In the 18th century, there was no way to record or play back music. If you wanted to listen to music, you had to pay a musician to play for you. The only people who could afford to do that were kings, queens and important people.

Leopold knew that it was unusual for someone as young as Wolfgang to be able to play as well as he did. He thought that people would be interested in hearing Wolfgang and his sister perform. To do this, the family would have to go travelling.

In 1762, when Wolfgang was six, the Mozart family travelled to Vienna to play for Empress Maria Theresa. Vienna was one of the most important cities in the world at the time. Mozart was so pleased to be there that he leapt on to the empress's lap and gave her a kiss!

Wolfgang played a mixture of music written by himself and other people. Everyone was impressed by Wolfgang's playing. The emperor called him a "little magician". Leopold decided to take his family to visit some more important people.

Wolfgang and Nannerl in their performance clothes

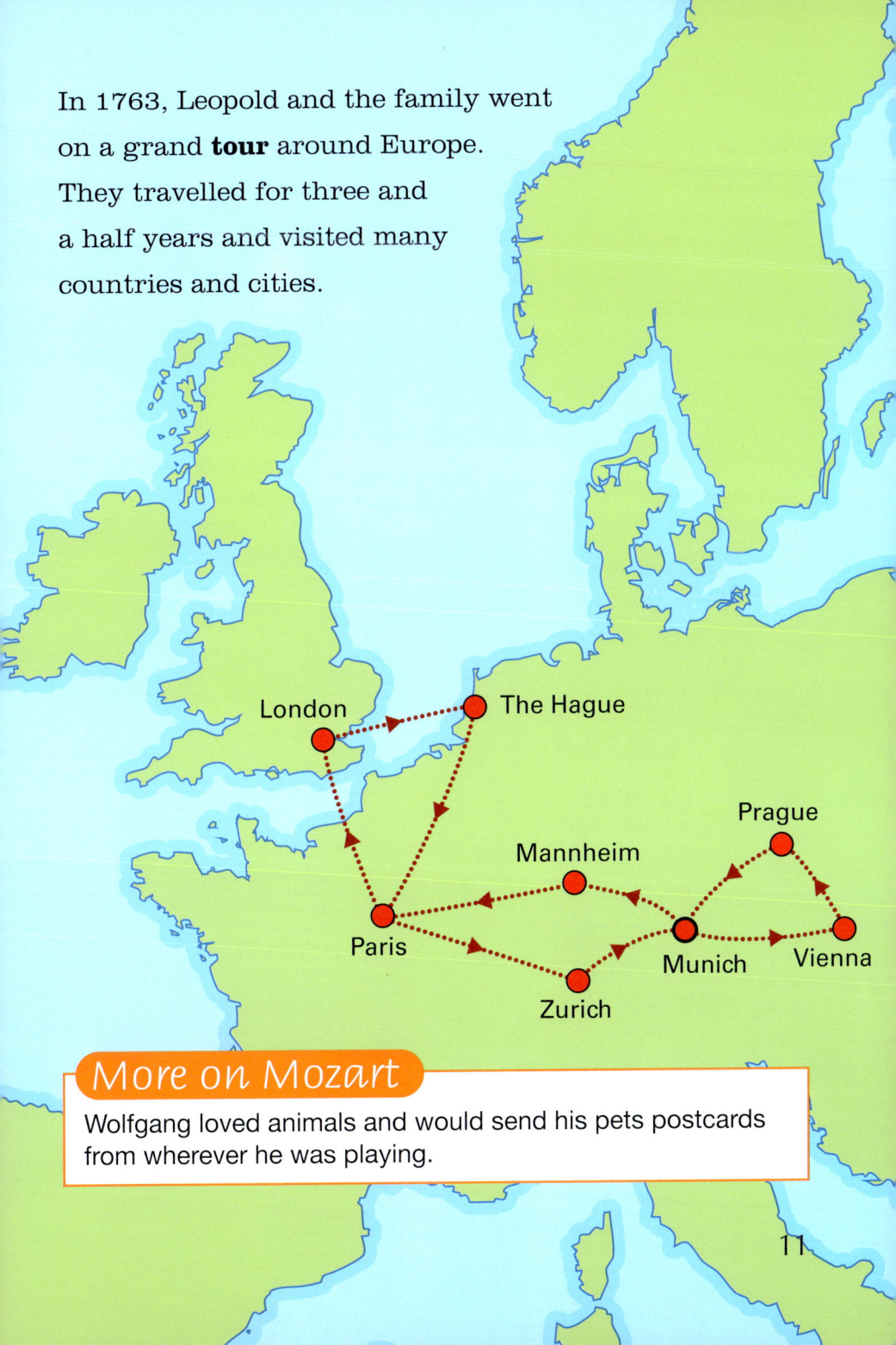

In 1763, Leopold and the family went on a grand **tour** around Europe. They travelled for three and a half years and visited many countries and cities.

More on Mozart

Wolfgang loved animals and would send his pets postcards from wherever he was playing.

Travelling in the 18th century took a long time and was very tiring. There were no cars or trains. The only way to travel was by horse and cart, or sometimes by boat. Nowadays, you can fly from Vienna to Paris in two hours; in those days it would take two weeks!

Wolfgang and Nannerl spent much of their childhood travelling and played for many important people. In London, Wolfgang played for King George III, and in Paris, he met Marie Antoinette, the future queen of France. He even asked her to marry him!

King George III

Marie Antoinette

When Wolfgang finally returned to Salzburg in 1773, he'd been travelling on and off for ten years.

While on tour, Wolfgang heard lots of different types of music. This helped him improve his own playing and composing. He also met composer Johann Sebastian Bach who encouraged Wolfgang to start writing symphonies.

Johann Sebastian Bach

13

Mozart's music

One of the things that made Mozart remarkable was the variety and amount of music he composed. Some of his most famous works are symphonies, concertos and operas.

A symphony is a long and complicated piece of music composed for a whole **orchestra**. He wrote his first one when he was only eight!

Mozart made another type of music, called a concerto, popular. A concerto is a piece of music composed for one instrument to be **accompanied** by an orchestra. He went on to compose many concertos for piano and violin.

Some of Mozart's most famous works are operas, which are plays set to music. Writing them was especially difficult for Mozart. Opera is an Italian art form and is traditionally performed in Italian, so Mozart had to write in a foreign language.

The Marriage of Figaro

Mozart covered lots of different themes with his operas. Some, such as The Marriage of Figaro (written in 1786) and Così Fan Tutte (1790), were funny. Some, such as Don Giovanni (1787), were dramatic. The Magic Flute (1791) is a fairy tale about a prince and princess. They are all still performed today.

More on Mozart

Mozart would hear music in his head and set it down on paper for others to play. He was writing music before he could write words, and his father would write the notes down for him.

Mozart usually only wrote music when he knew he would have an occasion to perform it, composing on his piano and sketching out musical ideas as he played along. When he thought he had something good, he would turn his ideas into a rough **score** so that others could play his music with him.

Sometimes Mozart didn't have enough time to write down his own part of the score. Instead, he would compose his own part on the spot, or play it from memory on the piano.

Doing things his way

In 1778, when Mozart was 22, his father thought his son had a better chance of becoming rich and famous in Paris. Wolfgang moved there with his mother, while Leopold stayed to work in Salzburg with Nannerl.

Sadly, his mother died and Wolfgang returned to Salzburg in 1779 to become a **court organist** and **concert master**.

In those days, to be paid to be a musician you had to be employed by a rich person or by the church. Because these people were paying you, they decided what music you played and composed.

Wolfgang wanted to make a living composing and playing his own music. In 1780, Wolfgang left his job and moved to Vienna to do things his way.

In Vienna, Wolfgang met Constanze Weber. They fell in love, but Wolfgang's father wouldn't give him permission to marry. He thought Wolfgang couldn't afford to marry without a proper job and a regular **wage**. Wolfgang disobeyed his father and in 1782 he married Constanze anyway.

Constanze Weber Mozart

Franz and Karl Mozart

Wolfgang and Constanze were very happy and had two sons. Sometimes they were very rich and sometimes they were very poor. It all depended on how well Mozart's composing was going. Mozart even worked as a music teacher to earn money.

More on Mozart

Once Wolfgang and Constanze were so cold, they burnt their furniture in the fire and danced around the room to keep warm.

Mozart's success

Some of Mozart's works were great successes and performed at the best opera houses in the world; others were not.

Mozart often struggled to make money and, over the course of his life, his fame and fortune went up and down. At the time of his death, Mozart was very poor indeed.

Mozart was well liked by other composers. Joseph Haydn was one of the most famous composers at the time. He was already famous when Mozart was a child and he thought Mozart was one of the best composers he'd ever heard.

Joseph Haydn

Ludwig van Beethoven

Ludwig van Beethoven was younger than Mozart, but respected him too. It's believed Beethoven travelled to Vienna to try and meet Mozart, but nobody knows if he ever did.

Mozart died in 1791. He was just 35 years old. The fact that he was so young when he died makes it even more remarkable that he composed so much music. He was buried in a **pauper's grave**, but his music was much loved.

Mozart is remembered on coins and stamps in Europe.

Other composers were **influenced** by his work and many still are today. A lot of famous people think Mozart is one of the finest composers that ever lived. Every January, there's a Mozart festival in Salzburg to celebrate Mozart's birthday. Thousands of visitors travel to Austria from all over the world to celebrate Mozart's life and music.

Glossary

accompanied   to serve as background music to another instrument

composer   a person who writes music

concert master   the best violinist in an orchestra who also acts as assistant to the composer

court organist   someone paid to play the organ for a king, queen or important person

harpsichord   a keyboard instrument in which strings are plucked

influenced   affected by someone or something

orchestra   a group of musicians playing different instruments to make music

pauper's grave   a grave that has to be paid for by the government because the family can't afford to pay

score   music written down to create a tune

tour   a journey to places to make music

wage   the money paid for doing a job

Index

Austria 2, 27
Bach, Johann Sebastian 13
Beethoven, Ludwig van 25
composer 2–3, 5, 13, 25, 27
concertos 14–15
Così Fan Tutte 17
Don Giovanni 17
Empress Maria Theresa 10
Europe 11
France 13
harpsichord 3, 6
Haydn, Joseph 25
King George III 13
London 13
Magic Flute, The 17
Marie Antoinette 13
Marriage of Figaro, The 17
Mozart, Anna Maria 4
Mozart, Leopold 4–6, 9–11, 20
Mozart, Maria Anna (Nannerl) 4–6, 13, 20
musicians 2, 4, 8, 21
operas 14, 16–17
orchestra 14–15
organ 6
Paris 12–13, 20
piano 15, 19
Salzburg 2, 13, 20, 27
score 19
symphonies 13–14
Vienna 10, 12, 21–22, 25
violin 6, 15
Weber, Constanze 22

Young Mozart's diary

Three years old

Today I began to play the harpsichord. Papa was very surprised at me!

Five years old

I am starting to write music and play more instruments, just like Papa. It's not difficult at all!

Eight years old

We are all in Vienna so I can perform in front of the emperor and empress. I've just written my first symphony!

Nine years old

Time to go on a tour of Europe! Travelling takes so long I can fit in writing a whole opera while we are moving from place to place.

Ideas for reading

Written by Clare Dowdall, PhD
Lecturer and Primary Literacy Consultant

Reading objectives:
- retrieve and record information from non-fiction
- discuss their understanding and explain the meaning of words in context
- ask questions to improve understanding
- draw inferences and justify these with evidence

Spoken language objectives:
- participate in discussions, presentations, performances, role play, improvisations and debates

Curriculum links: Music

Resources: Mozart's music, whiteboards, pens and pencils

Build a context for reading

- Ask children to name a famous musician. Explain that they are going to learn about a very famous musician from the 18th century: Mozart.
- Show them the front cover and ask children to describe what they can see, noting clues about the historical setting (costume, hair, furniture etc.).
- Read the blurb together. Help children to pronounce *Wolfgang Amadeus Mozart.*

Understand and apply reading strategies

- Based on the blurb, ask children to recount what Mozart's talent was, and to suggest how it was discovered.
- Read the contents and introduction together. Discuss what a *child genius* is and what a *composer* does, noticing the relationship to the word *compose.*
- Ask children to read to p6, looking for information about Mozart's genius and how it was discovered.